Pop Keyboard Intro

GW00536330

Since 1982 Great West Music has been successful in developing new and innovative music education programs that offer excellent curriculum for the teaching of popular music through the use of modern technology. The effectiveness of the programs has been proven through the popularity of the Technics Music Academy (T.M.A.) and continues to grow and provide legitimate, alternative music education today through Tritone Music Systems. These books will teach you how to play popular music on the piano or electronic keyboard through a simple, organized teaching approach. The instructions are easy to understand and the comprehensive method will ensure you understand all the concepts as you progress from song to song. We are confident that through the use of today's technology and this proven system you'll soon be experiencing the joy of making music.

Contents

Diagram Of The Keyboard And Notes

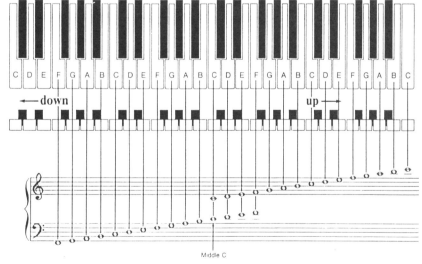

Middle C

Compiled and Edited by Merv Mauthe

HAL•LEONARD® CORPORATION
7777 W. BLUEMOUND RD. P.O. BOX 13819 MILWAUKEE, WI 53213

introducing...

Melody

All music is written on a staff made up of lines and spaces. In addition, some notes are written above or below the staff on short lines called leger lines.

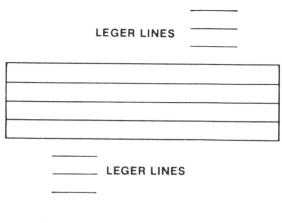

Every key on the keyboard is represented by a note placed on either a line or a space. The first five notes you will learn are C, D, E, F, G. Try finding the notes C, D, E, F, G on the keyboard.

To play a series of notes, or a melody, we will use our right hand on the keyboard and think of our fingers as being numbered from 1 to 5. Each finger will correspond to a different note. A treble clef 𝄞 appears at the beginning of each melody.

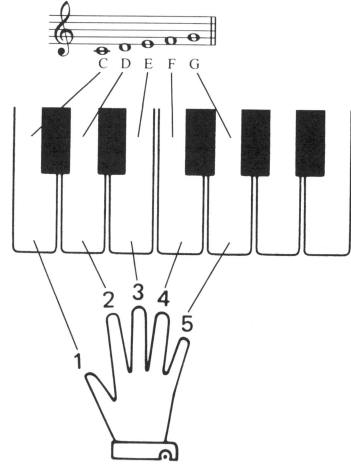

Try playing the melodies below. Finger numbers and note names have been shown to help you.

1	2	3	4	5	4	3	2	1
C	D	E	F	G	F	E	D	C

3	3	4	5	5	4	3	2	1
E	E	F	G	G	F	E	D	C

introducing...

Time Values

In order for music to have rhythm there are different types of notes that have a specific time value, or rhythmic beat. For example...

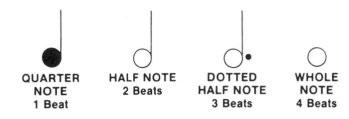

QUARTER NOTE — 1 Beat
HALF NOTE — 2 Beats
DOTTED HALF NOTE — 3 Beats
WHOLE NOTE — 4 Beats

Play the C's below holding each one for the proper number of beats.

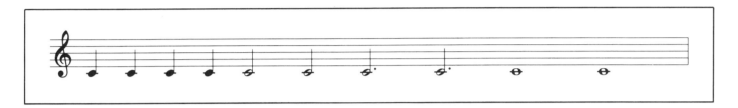

Once we have rhythm we can organize the staff into equal sections called measures or bars. A bar line separates each measure.

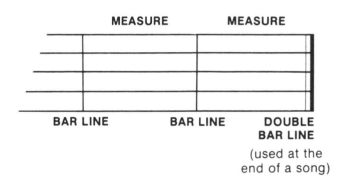

MEASURE   MEASURE

BAR LINE   BAR LINE   DOUBLE BAR LINE
(used at the end of a song)

At the beginning of each song, there is a set of numbers called a **time signature.** The time signature in your first few songs is $\frac{4}{4}$.

The **top** number indicates there are 4 beats in each measure.

The **bottom** number indicates that a quarter note receives one beat.

1   2   3   4   1   2   3   4

Play the melody below counting each beat and holding each note for its full time value. It will be using ♩ notes (1 count) and ♩ notes (two counts).

Time Signature:
4 beats in one measure
a quarter note gets 1 beat

Fingering:

Fingering:	3	3	4	5	5	4	3	2	1	1	2	3	3	2	2
Note names:	E	E	F	G	G	F	E	D	C	C	D	E	E	D	D
Beats:	1	2	3	4	1	2	3	4	1	2	3	4	1	2	3	4

Playing Tip:

An automatic rhythm unit or metronome can help keep a steady beat to your music and add a professional-sounding background.

introducing...

Accompaniment

Chords (a group of three or more notes played at the same time) provide the accompaniment for your melody. Chords are usually played with the left hand and are identified by chord symbols such as C, F and G7. They can also be notated on a staff that is usually preceded by a bass clef 𝄢 .

In your first song you will be using the two chords illustrated — C and G7. Find these two chords located to the left of middle C.

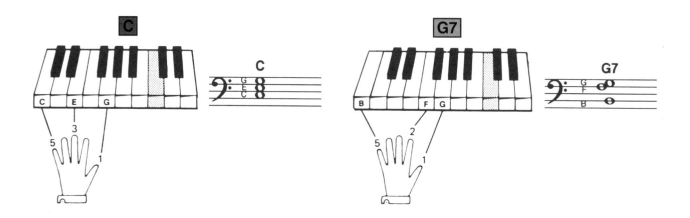

Play the sequence of chords below, holding each one for four beats.

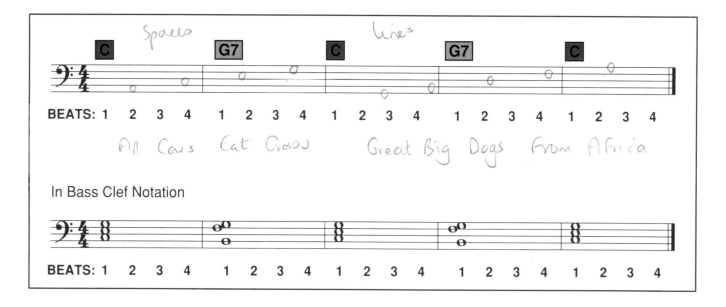

In Bass Clef Notation

Bass Clef Exercises

Practice the individual bass clef notes.

1.

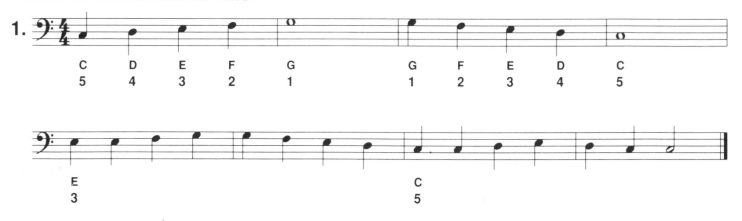

4

* Most standard music combines the treble and bass clefs in what is called the Grand Staff. The melody notes are written on the treble staff and the accompaniment notes are written on the bass staff.

Sound Set-Ups

The setting box at the beginning of each song encourages you to make full use of various effects and sounds and should be used or altered in whatever way best suits your instrument and musical tastes. Electronic pianos and keyboards are made up of a wide variety of orchestral sounds that range from traditional piano and strings to brass and percussive instruments. In addition, there are a variety of effects that can be added to the basic sound. The following songs provide you with a choice of three sound suggestions; however, feel free to experiment and be creative by selecting or "personalizing" the settings to meet your individual needs.

Performance Disks

To add more enjoyment to your musical experience, a performance disk of all the songs in this book is available. This disk contains a fully orchestrated performance of each song for listening and playing along. With the help of the disk arrangements you can learn the songs faster and sound more professional. Each hand is recorded separately (tracks 1 and 2) so you can practice individual parts at any speed while still benefiting from the background accompaniment. For those who have instruments with disk drive capability this is a great way to learn and play.

Ode To Joy

1  Piano   **2** Strings   **3** Organ

EFFECTS

Notes:

Rock or 8 beat ♩ = 90

Playing Tip:

* *A choice of 3 basic settings are provided for each song. Choose one that applies to your instrument or experiment with others of your choice. A suggested rhythm accompaniment and tempo have been included.*

* *Rhythms and tempos are only suggestions. Try all songs in a style and tempo you are comfortable with. Volume levels for the keyboard should be adjusted at your discretion.*

* *By practicing the melody and accompaniment separately first, you'll find it easier to put the two together.*

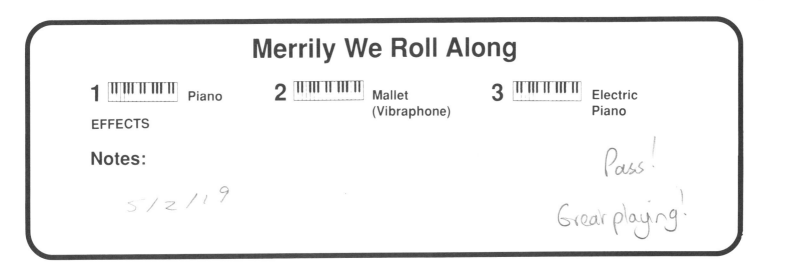

Merrily We Roll Along

Lightly Row

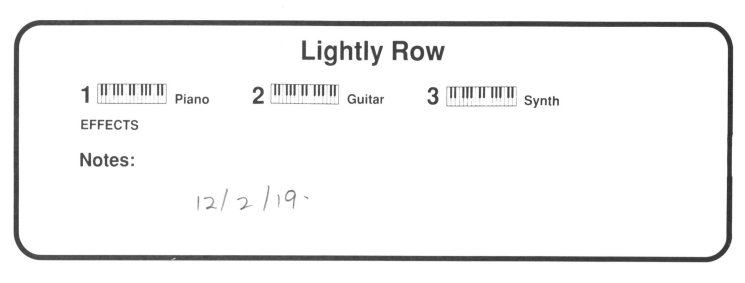

1 ▦ Piano   2 ▦ Guitar   3 ▦ Synth

EFFECTS

Notes:

12/2/19.

Review

12/2 In pencil

1. Write the letter name of each key marked with an **X**.

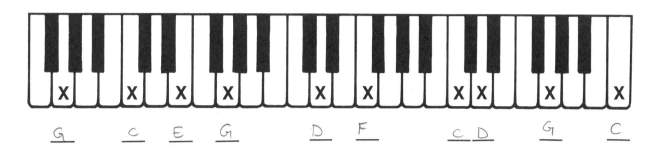

G   C   E   G   D   F   C D   G   C

✓

2. Name the Treble Clef notes.

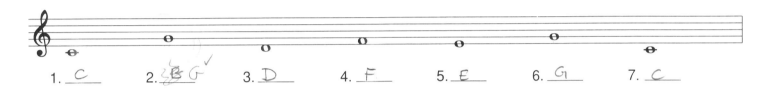

1. C   2. B G ✓   3. D   4. F   5. E   6. G   7. C

3. Name the Bass Clef notes.

1. C   2. G   3. F   4. D   5. E   6. C   7. B

4. Clap and count this rhythm pattern.

5. This note ♩ is a quarter note. The round part is filled in.

   Draw four quarter notes.

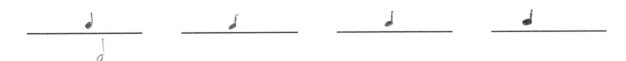

Perfect ✓

6. This note ♩ is a half note. The round part is not filled in.

   Draw four half notes.

introducing...

Ties

A curved line connecting two or more notes on the same line or space is called a tie. The first tied note is played and held for the total time value of all the tied notes.

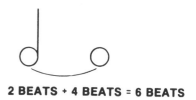

2 BEATS + 4 BEATS = 6 BEATS

A New Note

B is located to the left of C. Find some B keys on the keyboard.

The B we will be using in the next song is written slightly lower than C, just below the first leger line. Play it with your right thumb (1).

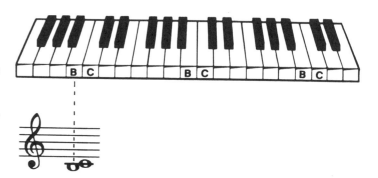

Exercise

Expression and Dynamics

Dynamics in music refers to the volume level. Certain symbols are used to indicate volume changes. Depending on the keyboard these can be achieved by either striking the key harder or softer, or through the use of an expression pedal.

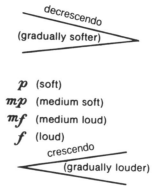

decrescendo
(gradually softer)

p (soft)
mp (medium soft)
mf (medium loud)
f (loud)

crescendo
(gradually louder)

Pick-up Notes

Many of the following songs have notes that start before the first complete measure of music. These are called pick-up notes and are usually played without rhythm or chord accompaniment. To indicate that no chord is played the letters N.C. appear above the melody notes.

Marianne

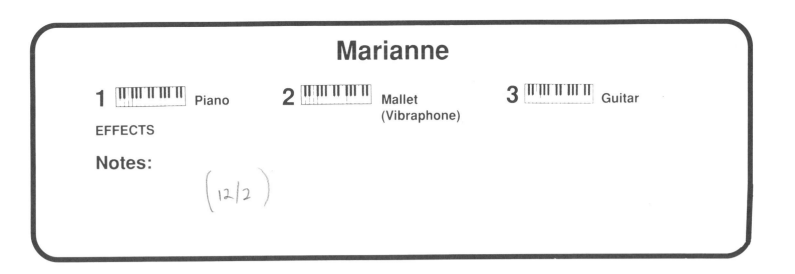

EFFECTS

Notes:　(12/2)

introducing...

The Dotted Half Note

When a dot is placed after a note, the time value of that note is increased by one half the original value. The dotted half note is held for three beats.

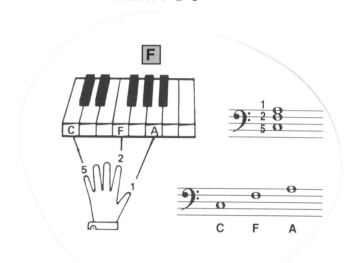

COUNT: 1 2 3

The F Chord

Find the F chord on the keyboard as illustrated. It contains the notes C, F, A and is located in the same general area as C and G7.

Chord Review

Practice the chords you know to this point in order to make changes quickly and accurately.

BEATS: 1 2 3 4 1 2 3 4 1 2 3 4 1 2 3 4 1 2 3 4 1 2 3 4 1 2 3 4 1 2 3 4

Bass Clef Exercise

Rests

When there is to be silence in music a rest is used. Rests have time values equal to their corresponding notes.

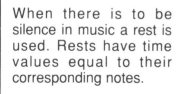

QUARTER REST - 1 BEAT

WHOLE REST - 4 BEATS
OR THE WHOLE MEASURE

HALF REST - 2 BEATS

When The Saints Go Marching In

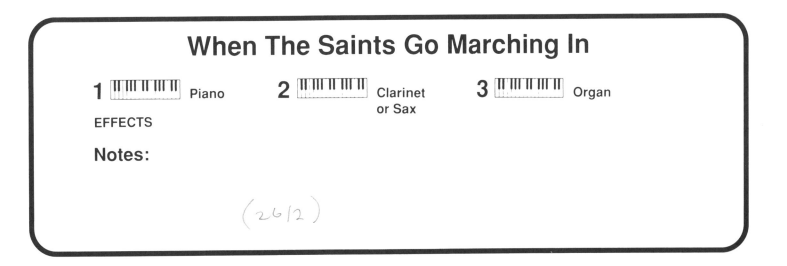

1 Piano   **2** Clarinet or Sax   **3** Organ

EFFECTS

Notes:

(26/2)

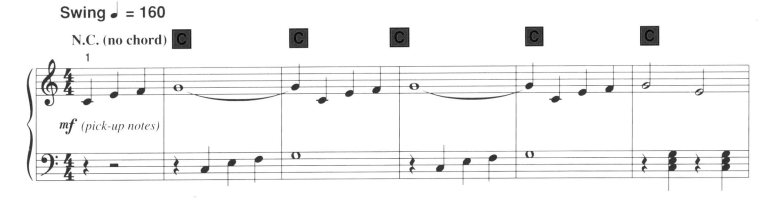

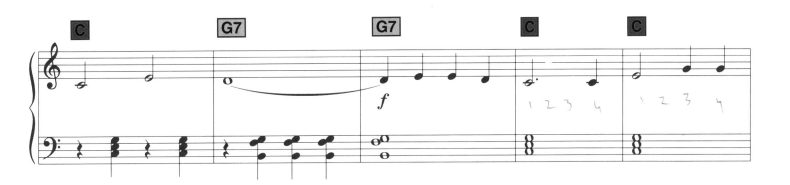

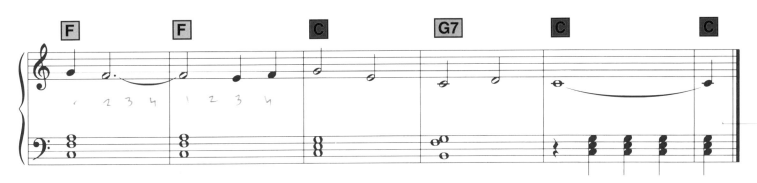

A New Time Signature

The next song you'll play is a waltz which has a time signature of $\frac{3}{4}$.
In this time signature there are three beats in each measure.

Beautiful Brown Eyes

1 Piano   2 Strings   3 Guitar

EFFECTS

Notes:

19/2/19.

Pass

3

broken chord

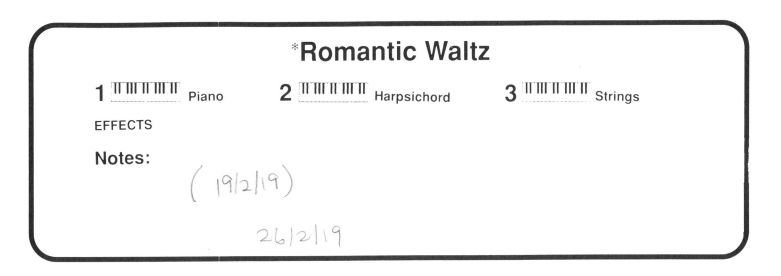

*Romantic Waltz

1 Piano 2 Harpsichord 3 Strings

EFFECTS

Notes:

(19/2/19)

26/2/19

(* To improve your left hand reading, this song contains no chord symbols.)

introducing...

A New Note

The A note is the white key located to the right of G. It is written in the second space.

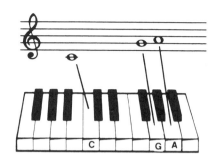

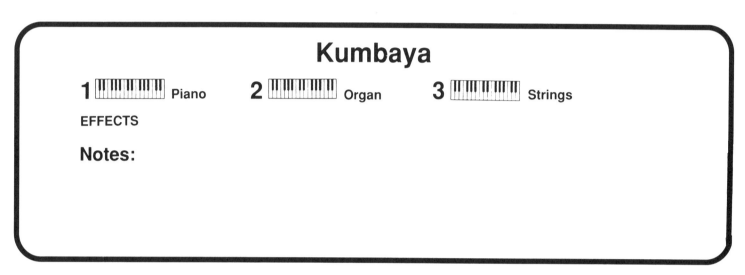

Kumbaya

1 Piano   2 Organ   3 Strings

EFFECTS

Notes:

8 beat or Disco ♩ = 100

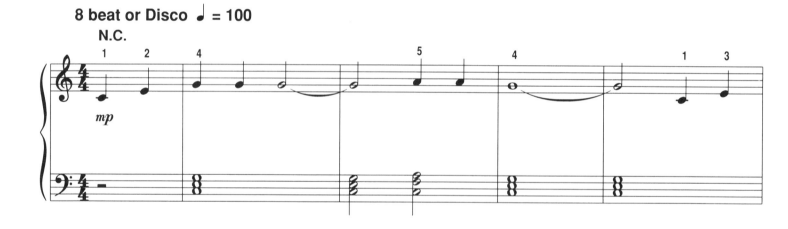

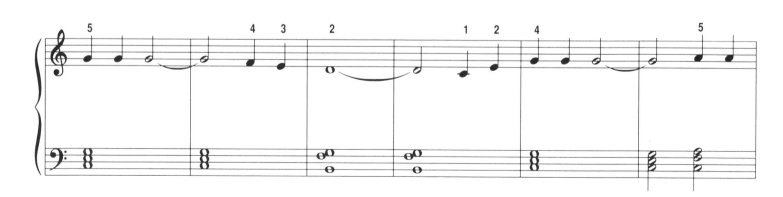

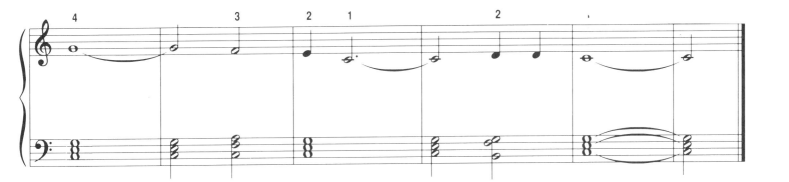

Review

1. Draw ten Treble Clef and ten Bass Clef signs on this Grand Staff.

2. The two numbers written at the beginning of music make up the _____.

3. A curved line which connects notes on the same line  or space _____ is called a _____.

4. Name these Treble Clef notes. Play them with your Right Hand.

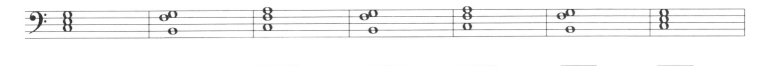

____ ____ ____ ____ ____ ____ ____

5. Name these Bass Clef chords. Play them with your Left Hand.

____ ____ ____ ____ ____ ____

6. Name these Bass Clef notes. Play them with your Left Hand.

____ ____ ____ ____ ____ ____

introducing...

Eighth Notes

A single eighth note has a flag on its stem and receives one half-beat.

Two or more eighth notes are connected by a beam.

To accurately play eighth notes say "and" between each beat.

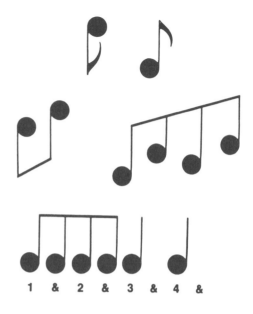

Dotted Quarter Notes

The dotted quarter note is held for one and a half beats, and is often followed by an eighth note.

Practice the dotted quarter notes and eighth notes using the melodies below.

LONDON BRIDGE

Swing or 8 beat ♩ = 120

LITTLE WALTZ

Waltz ♩ = 100

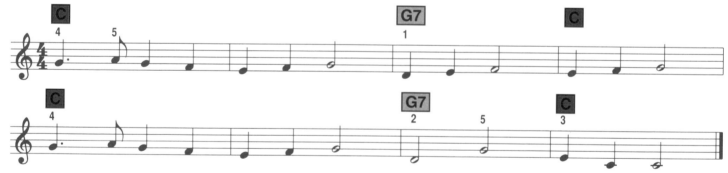

Michael, Row The Boat Ashore

1  Piano   **2** Guitar   **3** Electric Piano

EFFECTS

Notes:

introducing...

New Notes

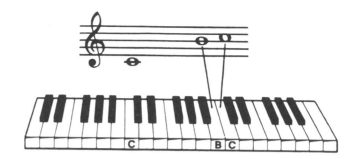

In the next two songs new B and C notes will be used. They are located to the right of A and are placed on the staff as shown.

Exercise

C Scale

Prep

Repeat Signs

When a song or portion of a song is to be repeated, this symbol appears. All the music within the repeat signs should be played again. When only one repeat is used, play the song again from the beginning.

Exercise

Step By Step

Shuffle ♩ = 100

1st and 2nd Endings

When two different endings appear play the song through to the first ending, repeat from the closest repeat sign or the beginning, skip the first ending and play the second ending.

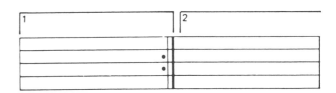

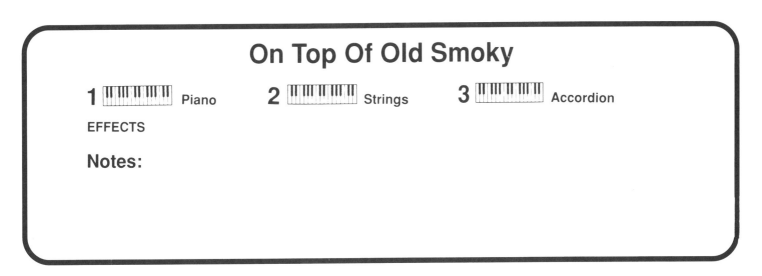

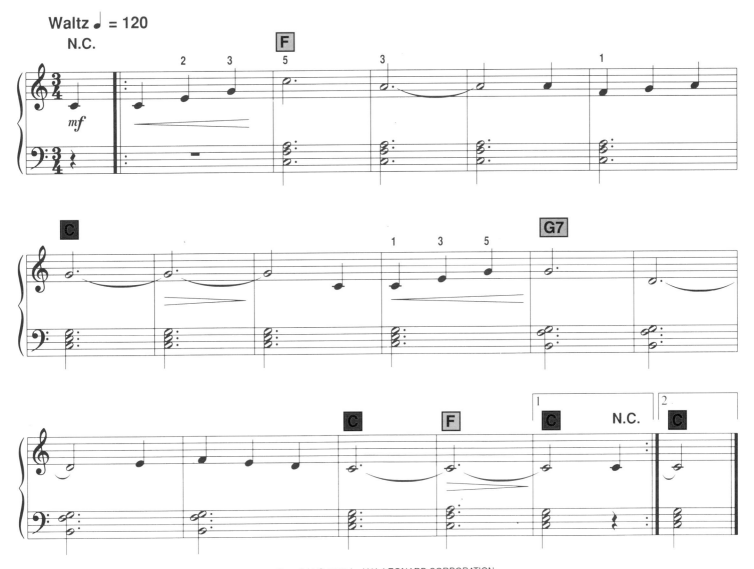

Tourelay, Tourelay

1 ▦ Piano **2** ▦ Guitar **3** ▦ Strings

EFFECTS

Notes:

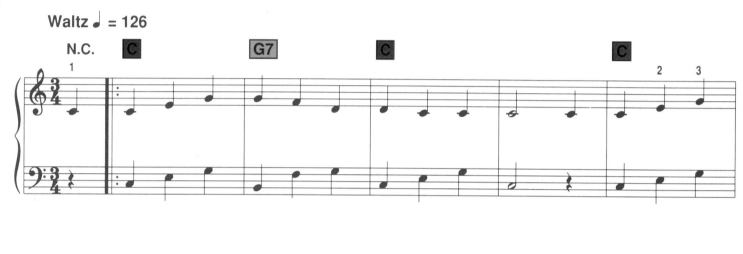

Bach Rock

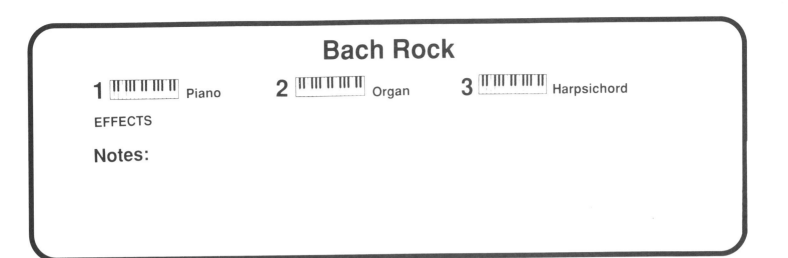

EFFECTS

Notes:

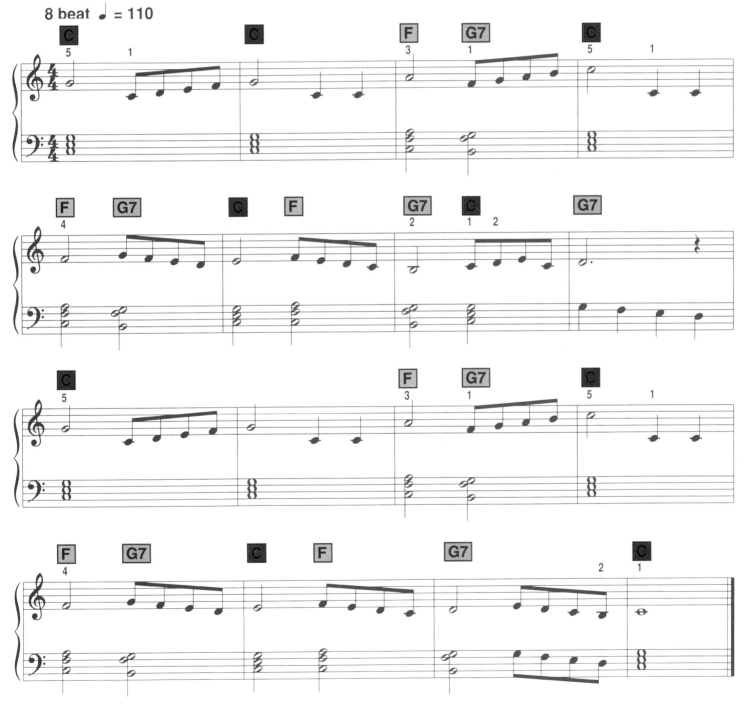

introducing...
New Notes

The next three songs use the new D, E and F notes. Notice their positions on the staff and their locations on the keyboard.

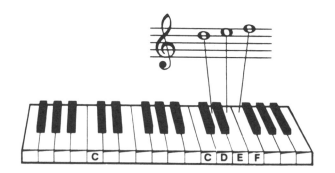

Swanee River

1 [keyboard] Piano **2** [keyboard] Guitar **3** [keyboard] Clarinet

EFFECTS

Notes:

Playing Tip:

Once you feel comfortable with the next song, try changing sounds at the ★. Setting 2 is suggested.

In the following songs, pay special attention to the fingering written above the notes.

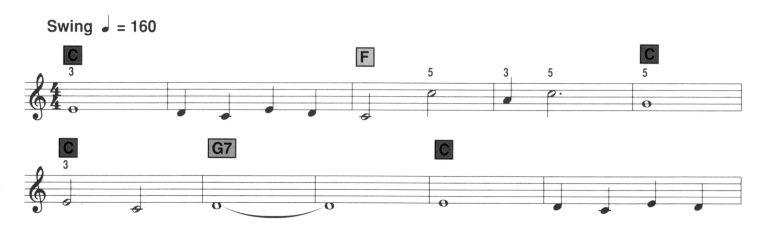

Review

Stems

* There are 5 staff lines.

* Notes that are **under** the middle line usually have stems going **up** on the **right** hand side.

* Notes that are **on or above** the middle line usually have stems going **down** on the **left** hand side.

* These points apply to treble clef and bass clef.

Add stems to these notes.

Draw the indicated single quarter notes (♩) on this staff. Play these notes.

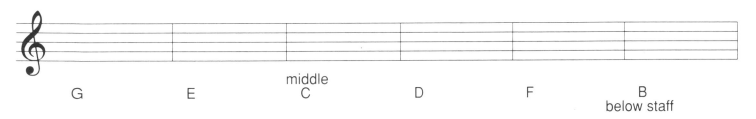

| G | E | middle C | D | F | B below staff |

Aura Lee

 **1** Piano
EFFECTS

 **2** Strings

3 Special (Vocal)

Notes:

Bossa nova ♩ = 100

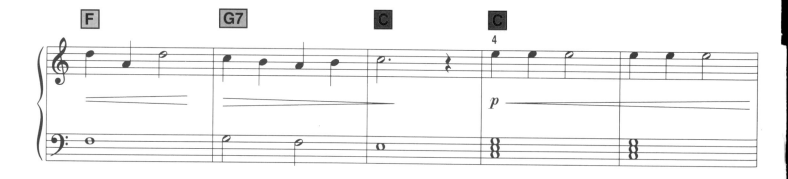

Vive L'Amour

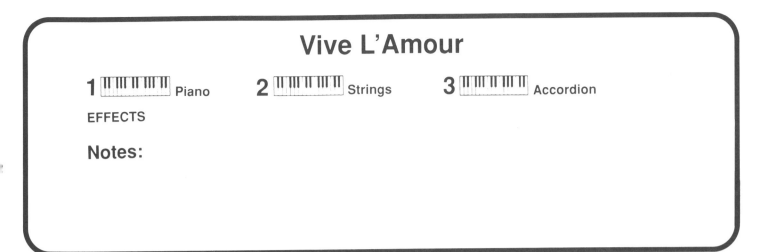

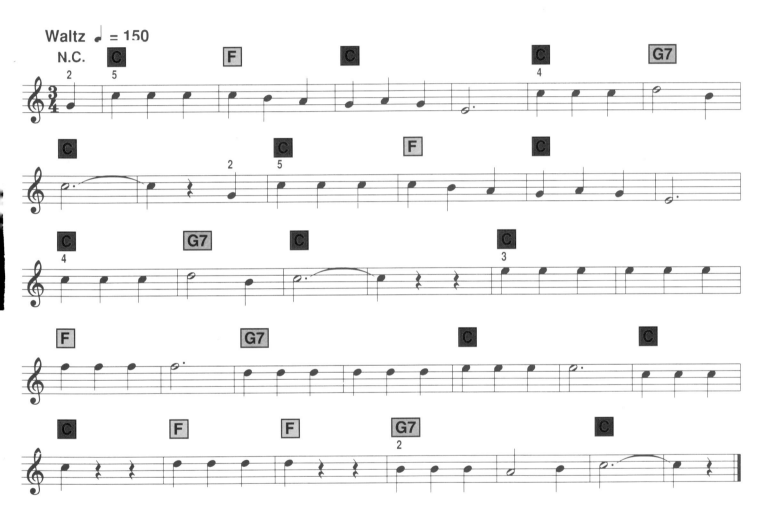

Accompaniment:

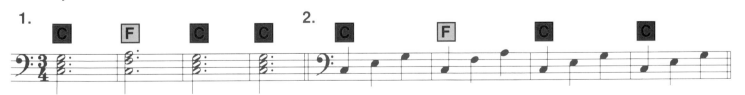

Basic Music Information

Symbol	Meaning	Symbol	Meaning
𝄞	Treble Clef	**N.C.**	No Chord
𝄢	Bass Clef	*p*	Piano (Softly)
4/4	Time Signature 4 Beats in a measure	*mp*	Mezzo Piano (Medium Soft)
3/4	Time Signature 3 Beats in a measure	*mf*	Mezzo Forte (Medium Loud)
o	Whole Note 4 Beats	*f*	Forte (Loud)
Whole Rest Whole Bar of Silence		Crescendo (Gradually Louder)	
♩. (dotted half)	Dotted Half Note 3 Beats	Decrescendo (Gradually Softer)	
♩ (half)	Half Note 2 Beats	First and Second Endings	
Half Rest 2 Beats Silence		Repeat Signs	
♩.	Dotted Quarter Note 1-1/2 Beats	Bar Lines and Measures	
♩	Quarter Note 1 Beat	Tie: Hold for the value of both notes	
Quarter Rest 1 Beat Silence			
♪	Eighth Note 1/2 Beat		

Congratulations

You've successfully completed the Intro level of the Pop Keyboard Course and are now ready to carry on to Grade 1 of the program. There you will learn dozens of new familiar songs, and gain more musical knowledge and ability through our organized and comprehensive system. Have fun!